# 30 DAYS
## TO OVERCOMING
## EMOTIONAL
## STRONGHOLDS

TONY EVANS

HARVEST HOUSE PUBLISHERS
EUGENE, OREGON

Unless otherwise indicated, Scripture quotations are from the New American Standard Bible®, © 1960, 1962, 1963, 1968, 1971, 1972, 1973, 1975, 1977, 1995 by The Lockman Foundation. Used by permission. (www.Lockman.org)

Verses marked NIV are taken from the Holy Bible, New International Version®, NIV®. Copyright © 1973, 1978, 1984, 2011 by Biblica, Inc.® Used by permission. All rights reserved worldwide.

*Cover by Dugan Design Group, Bloomington, Minnesota*

*Cover photo © Terry Dugan*

**30 DAYS TO OVERCOMING EMOTIONAL STRONGHOLDS**
Copyright © 2015 Tony Evans
Published by Harvest House Publishers
Eugene, Oregon 97402
www.harvesthousepublishers.com

ISBN 978-0-7369-6183-7 (pbk.)
ISBN 978-0-7369-6184-4 (eBook)

**Printed in the United States of America**

16  17  18  19  20  21  22  23  / BP-JH / 10  9  8  7  6  5  4

# CONTENTS

## Special Offer

Dr. Evans would like to share two
important messages with you that
will help you overcome fear and worry.

To download "Freedom from Fear"
(from Matthew 14:22-33) and "Be Happy,
Don't Worry" (from Philippians 4:6)
at no charge, visit our website:

**go.tonyevans.org/overcome**

# INTRODUCTION

Healthy emotions are to the soul what the senses are to the body. They reveal the way we feel about life's circumstances.

But some people are imprisoned by negative emotions. These people don't just have a bad day once in a while—that happens to all of us. Rather, they feel as if they're trapped, as if they can't escape, and as if their very life is being choked out of them. When they wake up in the morning, they don't say, "Good morning, Lord." Rather, they say, "Good Lord, it's morning." They struggle to survive and may feel helpless, hopeless, and worthless.

I use the word "stronghold" because anger, depression, worry, stress, low self-esteem…these are spiritual issues. They must be overcome spiritually. When we get the spiritual component right, we won't be enslaved by our emotions.

Some emotional strongholds can be tied to a physiological cause, such as a chemical imbalance. But most emotional strongholds don't spring from physiological causes. Rather, they stem from sin—either your own or someone else's. For example, you might struggle with emotions of guilt, shame, or regret because of wrong choices you have made. Or you may have suffered abuse, rape, betrayal, or rejection. In these cases, the stronghold of fear, insecurity, or worry didn't come from your own sin but from others'.

Emotional strongholds can even result from what I call "atmospheric sin." This happens when sin clouds the atmosphere around us and affects us regardless of whether we actively participate in it. This is often the case with greed, social irresponsibility, injustice, racism, and so on. These can lead to emotional strongholds just as secondhand smoke can lead to lung cancer. In an environment that is rife with sin, people are more likely to suffer from emotional strongholds.

People who find themselves enslaved to their emotions may deny the problem exists, or they may use pills, entertainment, sex, or money to distract themselves from the real issues causing their emotional discomfort. But I want to help you discover the root behind what you are experiencing so you can overcome it. I want to look beyond your feelings so you can discover and address the causes of your emotional strongholds—and overcome them.

God did not create you to be imprisoned by emotional strongholds. Rather, He has promised you a full life in Christ. Jesus said, "I came that they may have life, and have it abundantly" (John 10:10). He has not called you to live each day in defeat. He wants you to know and trust that He is in control of all things and that He is watching over your entire life.

If you are not experiencing the abundant life Christ freely gives, now is the time to overcome your emotional strongholds. Turn to Him and ask Him to reveal the areas where an emotional stronghold may have set in. He wants to show you how to see past your sorrow—how to view your life from His vantage point.

From where you stand right now, life may look dismal. Yet from where God is seated, all is well. When we overcome emotional strongholds, we let go of our need to understand everything right now. We trust God to make a miracle out of what looks like a mess.

Remember, emotions don't think—they merely respond. Emotions have to borrow thoughts in order to stimulate feelings from them. Therefore, whatever controls your thoughts also controls how you feel.

For example, if you were weighed down with worry and stress because your bills had piled up, you had been laid off from work, and you saw no way out of your financial chaos, your emotions would be responding to how you were thinking about your situation.

But if I handed you a check for $500,000…well, let's just say your emotions would completely change. That's because your emotions follow your thoughts. You can overcome emotional strongholds by mastering your thinking. When you align your thoughts with God's truth, you will be set free. Guaranteed.

# WEEK ONE
## EMOTIONS

### DAY ONE

The battle to overcome your emotional strongholds is a battle for your mind. Whoever and whatever controls your mind controls your emotions (and your actions). So if you are worrying, stressed out, and depressed, you're probably thinking things that aren't true. That's why the apostle Paul tells us we don't war against the flesh, but against Satan's attacks on our mind.

> The weapons of our warfare are not of the flesh, but divinely powerful for the destruction of fortresses. We are destroying speculations and every lofty thing raised up against the knowledge of God, and we are taking every thought captive to the obedience of Christ (2 Corinthians 10:4-5).

So we're fighting not only our flesh but also our minds—and Satan's lies. One of Satan's favorite strategies is to plant his thoughts in our minds, disguising them as our own thoughts. We accept them as true and begin to act on them. This is the same strategy he used with Eve in the garden when he twisted God's truth and enticed her to sin.

But if Satan is sending us these sinful thoughts, how can we be blamed for thinking them or acting on them? The answer is that you and I are responsible for what we do with these thoughts once they enter our minds. That's why the passage we just looked at says we are to take every thought captive to the obedience of Christ.

When a thought enters your mind, luring you into an emotional stronghold of worry, doubt, anger, hate, or shame, you have two choices. You can reject the thought, or you can adopt it and make it your own. By rejecting it, you tear down the stronghold and put an end to the false way of thinking. It can't dominate or corrupt your emotions any longer.

Paul says our thoughts can lead in two directions. "For the mind set on the flesh is death, but the mind set on the Spirit is life and peace" (Romans 8:6). In this verse, "death" is the opposite of life and peace. It is spiritual impoverishment—you may be alive physically, but your emotional life is ebbing away. This ebbing away leads to worry and depression because the flesh does not bring peace, joy, or purpose.

On the other hand, if you set your mind on the things of the Spirit, you have life and peace, purpose and meaning, hope and joy. When the Holy Spirit governs your thoughts, external circumstances don't dictate your responses.

So if you want to overcome emotional strongholds, *change your thoughts*. To break free from whatever is holding you hostage, reject Satan's attempts to influence your thoughts and set your mind on God's truth—what He says about you and your circumstances.

## DAY TWO

The best ways to begin overcoming emotional strongholds are to understand your identity in Christ and to avoid a life of sin.

Worry, fear, doubt, hate…all of these and more overtake us when we don't remember who we are in Christ. On the other hand, when we focus on the truth about our identity in Him, we enjoy new life.

> What shall we say, then? Are we to continue in sin so that grace may increase? May it never be! How shall we who died to sin still live in it? Or do you not know that all of us who have been baptized into Christ Jesus have been baptized into His death? Therefore we have been buried with Him through

baptism into death, so that as Christ was
raised from the dead through the glory of
the Father, so we too might walk in newness
of life (Romans 6:1-4).

Take a look in the mirror. That person you see was
crucified, buried, and resurrected with Christ. When
Jesus died 2000 years ago, so did you. When He was
buried, you lay in the tomb with Him. When He rose,
you did too. You may have received Christ only a short
time ago, but those events in Jesus' life form the foundation of your spiritual identity.

How does this identification work? The process
reminds me of the jumper cables I keep in my car. Once
a good battery is connected to a dead battery, the car can
be started. Electrical current flows from the good battery
into the dead battery. Through no action of its own, the
dead battery becomes "alive" again.

In the first century, Jesus defeated sin and death with
all the power necessary to jump-start those who are dead
in sin. Like a set of jumper cables, the Holy Spirit con-
nects your dead soul with Jesus' victory on the cross. The
result: Your spirit "turns over," and you are raised to walk
in newness of life.

This is why you *can* overcome your emotional strongholds. I know you can because I know who you are in
Christ.

Satan is a master at disguising his thoughts as your

own. *I can't overcome worry...I can't be free from this emotional bondage...I can't resist these old habits of falling into depression...* In order to overcome, you must *stop believing these lies*. Those statements may have been true when the *old* you was alive. But that person died on the cross with Christ. You are a completely new creation (2 Corinthians 5:17).

Consider the electric appliances in your kitchen. They all draw power from the same source. If your house has no electricity, none of those appliances will work. Likewise, people who are not connected to Christ are powerless to overcome their emotional strongholds. But those who belong to Christ are plugged into the same unlimited power source. The same power that enabled someone else to overcome a stronghold is available to you. Christ is in the business of setting people free. You cooperate with Him by acknowledging that your new life in Him empowers you to overcome every lie the enemy plants in your mind. You have the power to overcome whatever is holding you down.

One day many decades ago, Sir Frederick Handley Page—a pioneer in aviation—was flying one of his planes across a barren Middle Eastern desert, unaware that a large rat had crawled into the cargo hold behind the cockpit before takeoff. While cruising several thousand feet, Page heard the sickening sound of gnawing from behind him. His heart began to pound—hydraulic lines and control cables ran throughout the cargo area.

One misplaced bite could disable the aircraft and send him to his death.

Autopilot did not yet exist, so being alone, Page couldn't abandon the controls momentarily to deal with his uninvited guest. Descending from his current altitude and landing might take too long. Besides, touching down on the desert sand was risky, and his chances of being able to take off again were even slimmer.

That's when Page recalled a piece of trivia: Rats require more oxygen to survive than do humans. Page pulled back on the yoke, and the aircraft climbed. In a few short moments, the gnawing sound stopped. Safely on the ground a few hours later, Page discovered a dead rat lying just behind the cockpit.

Friend, Satan can't live in the atmosphere of God's truth. His dark lies fade away in the light of God's presence. Soar in the heavenlies by aligning your thinking with God's perspective (see Ephesians 2:6). Sure, the air might be a little thin if you're not used to it, but the Spirit will sustain you.

Keep climbing into God's mindset and adopting His perspective until He brings the victory you thought was impossible. Rehearse the truth over and over until Satan and his emotional strongholds fall to the floor and die for lack of air. When they do, you will breathe free.

## DAY THREE

Emotional strongholds tend to fall into three categories. The first category includes strongholds rooted in your past. For example, you may have been traumatized during your developmental years. Perhaps you experienced times of neglect early on—a lack of love, esteem, or companionship. You might have suffered abuse.

This category also includes things that occurred as recently as last month. Your choices as an adult might have triggered difficult consequences and deep regret. In either case, an emotional groove was formed, and you have adopted it as your normal way of thinking and looking at life.

The second category of emotional strongholds includes things happening right now. You might be facing trials and tests that are causing emotional fatigue and distress. Perhaps your work environment is unstable, your boss is demanding, or you are in a difficult relationship. Your health may have taken a turn for the worse, or your child might be beginning to rebel. Challenges like these can attack your emotional stability. Looking for comfort from food, illicit relationships, or any other quick fix can make the situation even worse.

The third category of emotional strongholds involves the future. This is most easily summed up by the word "worry." Worry is one of the most common strongholds for many people. You ask yourself questions like these: *What if I get cancer? What if my husband has a heart attack? What if one of my children cuts or drinks or dies? What if we lose our retirement funds or have to foreclose on our mortgage? What if our marriage doesn't make it after all these years—what then?*

People who worry about the future become paralyzed today. In the Bible, Queen Esther had every reason to be held hostage to a fear of the future. The king had decreed the annihilation of all Jews—which, unbeknownst to him, included her. Regardless, Esther did not cower under a fear of the future. Rather, she walked victoriously in the present. She was afraid, yes. But her courage overcame her fear. And her wisdom led her to ask her friends and family to pray for her.

What triggers most of your emotional strongholds—difficulties in your past? Trials in your present? Fears of your future? Or all three? When you identify the source of your strongholds, you can isolate the lies, replace them with God's truth, and be set free.

## DAY FOUR

Have you ever asked yourself whom or what you could not live without? Some people may make a list of material things. Others may say they couldn't live without their spouse. Still others would think of the deep friendships they've formed.

All these are wonderful, God-given blessings. However, I believe we mix up our values when we assign greater worth to things and people than to God. When we do that, we become codependent on the gifts God has given us.

Codependency is a destructive coping mechanism (one form of an emotional stronghold) that people use to deal with a lack they may feel. Perhaps they lack self-esteem or have strong feelings of rejection. Regardless, codependent people usually use others to fix what is broken in themselves. They look to others to fill their own emptiness. I call this a "people stronghold."

God is the only One who can fix what is broken. Only Jesus can meet all our needs. We cause problems when we turn to other people before we turn to Him. Throughout His Word we see God using people in the lives of others, but He never allows people or things to take His place. When we let that happen, we have created an emotional idol.

When you receive good news that fills your heart with joy, do you pick up the phone to call a friend, or do you take time to thank the One who has sent the blessing? When trials come and the storms of life crash down around you, do you immediately cry out to your spouse, or do you cry out to God first? If you will begin going to God first, your dependence on Him will increase and your codependence on others will decrease. Find your encouragement in Him, and He will also send you waves of encouragement through those you love.

Use these steps to break free from codependence.

1. When your mind wanders to someone else more than it should, shift your thoughts to God and His Word.

2. Intentionally seek out ways to have fun— activities you enjoy, not activities you think others will enjoy or activities that depend on others.

3. Pay attention to how you talk about yourself. Do you put yourself down? Do you let others put you down? Change this pattern by affirming the positive things God is doing in your life. Use words that build up and don't tear down.

4. Let go of the need to control situations and the people around you.

5. Create a list of your positive attributes and thank God for them. Read through this list daily and add to it often.

6. Gradually reduce your texts and conversations with those on whom you may be codependent.

7. Write yourself notes of affirmation and leave them where you'll see them. Send yourself positive emails. Buy yourself flowers or tickets to a sports

event to remind yourself of the value God places on you.

## DAY FIVE

When a basketball player has a tough time in his game, we say he's in a slump. This is not unusual—athletes go through slumps all the time. They don't panic, but they can't just stay there. At some point, they have to rebound. They have to bounce back.

Being bound by an emotional stronghold can be akin to living in a slump. You aren't able to accomplish things the way you normally can, you don't enjoy the experiences you were made to enjoy, and you don't feel as if you're fulfilling the purpose God has destined for you. You're still on the team—you're in God's family— but you're not living up to your potential. Falling into a slump from time to time is normal, but remaining there is not. You must be about the business of getting out.

Many of God's best servants experienced slumps, and their stories reveal some principles of how they got out and how we can get out as well. Moses, the man who eventually delivered Israel from hundreds of years of bondage, parted the Red Sea, brought us the Ten Commandments, and wrote the first five books of the Bible, found himself in a slump—the first of several. His own choices contributed to this first slump, but I want to look at the powerful way he got out of it.

Moses' initial problem had to do with people. He was hit hard by feelings of rejection. Perhaps you can identify. Maybe you've experienced rejection and are suffering from its effect—low self-esteem. If so, take heart because Moses has been where you are, and he was able to overcome.

Moses' problems began at about age 40 when he saw an Egyptian beating a Hebrew and decided to intervene on behalf of the Hebrew (Acts 7:24-25). When he killed the Egyptian and hid the body, he thought his Hebrew people would understand that he was there to deliver them, but they did not. Instead, they feared him and subsequently rejected him (Exodus 2:13-14).

In fact, Moses was rejected not only by his own people but also by the Egyptians, including his own adopted family. As a result, Moses fled from Egypt. For 40 more years Moses stayed in a foreign land, and we witness a distinct change in his confidence during this time. The once self-assured man who was going to free the Israelite people all by himself, one Egyptian at a time, no longer had any confidence at all.

Moses was experiencing the emotional stronghold of low self-esteem. We see this most clearly in Moses' encounter with God at the burning bush.

God gives Moses his marching orders. "Therefore,

come now, and I will send you to Pharaoh, so that you may bring My people, the sons of Israel, out of Egypt" (Exodus 3:10).

Great—it's finally time for Moses to fulfill his calling! He should be ecstatic! *Wrong.* Moses' reply reveals anything but joy. "Who am I, that I should go to Pharaoh, and that I should bring the sons of Israel out of Egypt?" (verse 11).

In other words, Moses didn't feel worthy of his purpose and his destiny. He lacked a sense of personal worth, and he lacked confidence in his skills. Later on in his dialogue with God, Moses asks, "What if they will not believe me or listen to what I say?" (Exodus 4:1).

God told Moses to throw down the staff in his hand. When Moses did so, it became a snake. God then told Moses to pick it back up by its tail, and when he did, it became his staff again. God showed Moses that even though his own personal strength was insufficient, he would be able to carry out his destiny in God's strength and power. It wasn't up to Moses to be "all that"—it was up to God.

The same is true for you. The weight of fulfilling your destiny and becoming all you were created to be isn't on your shoulders. It's on God's.

When you trust Him and His power and let go of what has you bound, you will experience the confidence you need to fulfill your destiny. Your esteem should never be based on who you are or what you can do, but rather in the power God can manifest in and through you. In Him, you can do all things (Philippians 4:13). Let that truth take root in your heart and give you great confidence.

## DAY SIX

Have you been rejected? Do you feel as if you're not worthy to be commissioned by God? The good news is that you can overcome feelings of rejection and unworthiness because you are not on your own. You don't have to look to yourself for a sense of worth. You can look to God, your Creator.

When Moses experienced rejection and fell into an emotional stronghold of low self-esteem, God responded to Moses' lack of personal power by revealing His own power. God longs to reveal His power to you too. That happens when you let go of what you know (just as Moses let go of the shepherd's staff he had depended on for so long) and pick back up what God has anointed. Put your focus on what He can do, not on what you have done or what has happened to you.

If you're suffering from rejection, remember these three things.

1. Your greatest need is not self-confidence—it's confidence in God.

2. God uses our difficult experiences to prepare us for future ministry and blessing.

3. Obeying God leads to a new, accurate image of yourself.

Read the first few chapters of Exodus. As you empathize with Moses, you'll see that you can get back up and start over—in God's strength, not your own. And friend, notice what you're holding in your hand. Whatever it is, *throw it down*. Let God touch it. Then pick it back up again. With God, you can overcome.

Remember what we've looked at this week. We start breaking free from emotional strongholds when we increase our awareness and change our thinking. Ignoring our strongholds or denying they exist only make matters worse. You can't overcome emotional strongholds simply by wishing them away. You may be able to distract yourself from your strongholds temporarily, but that won't bring about a cure. In fact, such distractions as eating, spending, drinking, sex, and entertainment can lead to even more strongholds!

You also can't overcome your stronghold by giving in to it. You may feel like cutting, swearing, drinking, spending, or simply withdrawing from those around you, but those things won't help you overcome. They will merely mask your pain as you sink deeper into emotional bondage.

Your key to victory is to acknowledge and address the root—the lies you have been tricked into thinking are true. When Satan influences your thought life, you feel whatever he wants you to feel. When God dominates your thought life, you feel what God designed you to feel.

The way you respond to events in your life often reveals what you believe. For example, if you doubt in your heart that God sees when you're wronged, that He cares when you're hurt, or that He has your best interest in mind, you'll try to rectify your situation yourself rather than trusting Him and His ways.

Friend, God saw what happened to you, what is happening to you, or what you're afraid may happen to you. Trying to take care of things our own way only compounds the problem and inhibits His response and deliverance.

God is the One who will tear down your emotional stronghold if you will let Him. He is in control. He hears. He knows. He sees. He cares. Trust Him and move on.

## DAY SEVEN

### Prayers and Practicals

*Dear Father, I've been bound by my emotions
for too long. I've suffered as they have directed
and dictated my life. I've wasted too much
time on worry, regret, fear, or shame. Lord,
lead me in the path that brings wisdom and
understanding. Free me from the chains of
my past that are wrapped around my mind.
Show me the goodness that comes from trusting
in what You say. You have already won my
victory—now grant me the grace to live it out.*

#### Prayer Needs and Requests

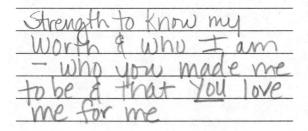

Strength to know my
worth & who I am
— who you made me
to be & that You love
me for me

*My Own Prayer*

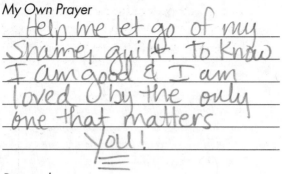

Help me let go of my
shame, guilt. To know
I am good & I am
loved by the only
one that matters
you!

*Practicals*

1. People with emotional strongholds often
   struggle with codependence. Seek to establish
   new relationships and interests. As you develop
   appropriate emotional attachments with more
   people and activities, you will learn to depend
   on God instead of others, and your sense of your
   personal worth will grow.

2. Replace rejection with affirmation. Rejection
   is an ego-reducing emotion we have all faced.
   Affirmation feeds the core of who you are with
   the spiritual truth of how God sees you and
   accepts you. Write the following verses on your
   phone, tablet, sticky notes, computer...wherever
   you will see them and memorize them: Psalms
   37:23-24 and 139:14; Isaiah 41:10; Jeremiah 29:11;
   John 14:27; Ephesians 2:10; and Hebrews 13:6.

3. Throw it down. Identify the thing, person, or experience from your past that ties you to your emotional stronghold. This could be a habit or something you depend on more than God. Go before the Lord and let it go, asking Him to anoint you and replace it with His power and strength.

# WEEK TWO

## STRESS

## DAY ONE

Everyone deals with stress. Each of us handles it differently, and some of us can't handle it at all. No one is exempt from its presence or its effects.

I visited the doctor recently for a checkup. The doctor found nothing wrong with my test results. The problem, he said, was me. He could see signs of stress in my face and body language. Yes, I admit it—I struggle with stress myself. I suspect that most pastors do.

I suspect you're no stranger to stress either. Perhaps you face stress in your marriage, with your kids, or at work.

One of the major causes of stress is having too much on our plate—trying to accomplish too much or fit too much into our already crowded schedule. Our attempts to restructure our lives and alleviate stress can become so complicated and time consuming that we create more pressure than we relieve.

When that happens, our lives can start to resemble

a stacking puzzle. We pile one demand or responsibility atop another until we're gazing at a mountain of stress. No wonder the whole thing sometimes comes crashing down. Anything that threatens to upset the delicate balance of our lives or to slow our frantic pace can become yet another source of stress and frustration. This includes healthy, important things, such as engaging in church life or building relationships.

Single parents face unimaginable stress. A mother raising children alone must pursue excellence on the job, only to come home and cook meals, clean the house, help with homework, provide spiritual leadership, and offer emotional support and nurture. And that's before she even *thinks* about herself and her needs.

Stress is everywhere, and unfortunately it's become one of the major emotional strongholds facing us today. More than 75 percent of adults recently surveyed by the American Psychological Association reported experiencing moderate to high levels of stress in the past month. Eighty percent admitted to feeling stress on the job, and approximately one out of every 75 people suffers from panic attacks (most often brought on by stress).

Ongoing stress damages the body. It can fuel cancer cells, encourage chronic health conditions, raise the risk of heart attacks, and more. Overcoming the emotional stronghold of stress may do more than brighten your days—it may prolong them.

But how do we overcome the stress in our lives?

God's answer is found in what I sometimes call the "epistle on pressure"—Paul's letter to the church at Philippi. Paul dictated this letter in a Roman prison, awaiting a verdict on crimes he did not commit. Most of us would consider this a high-stress situation. The congregation at Philippi was in a different sort of pressure cooker. It was torn by conflict between two women (Philippians 4:2-3) and by pressure from the community (Philippians 1:27-30).

Paul gave three simple ingredients to overcoming stress, the first of which we'll look at today. While confined in prison, waiting to hear whether he would live or die, Paul wrote, "Rejoice in the Lord always; again I will say, rejoice!" (4:4).

Excuse me? Did Paul just write to rejoice in the Lord as he sat chained in prison awaiting a verdict of life or death? Yes, he did.

The only source of victory over stress is God. Or, to paraphrase this passage, we must find our *chief joy* in the Lord. Nothing is wrong with being made happy by your mate, your job, your home, your car, or a variety of other things. All of these things can produce some happiness. But happiness is different from joy. Happiness depends on circumstances, but joy transcends them.

For example, if you'll take a moment to read the book of Habakkuk (it's only three chapters long), you will see a man responding in joy despite the most terrible circumstances. We read of anguish, loss, and even silence from God. We see Habakkuk's discouragement, depression, and difficult circumstances. But in the end, we also read this:

> Though the fig tree should not blossom and there be no fruit on the vines, though the yield of the olive should fail and the fields produce no food, though the flock should be cut off from the fold and there be no cattle in the stalls, yet I will exult in the LORD, I will rejoice in the God of my salvation. The Lord GOD is my strength, and He has made my feet like hinds' feet, and makes me walk on my high places (Habakkuk 3:17-19).

Real joy has nothing to do with how things are going. Joy is a question of your state of being *regardless of how things are going.* Joy has to do with a God-given, internal ability to cope. It can produce peace in the midst of panic, calm in the midst of chaos, and tranquility in the midst of turmoil. The first step to overcoming the emotional stronghold of stress is to make a conscious choice to rejoice.

## DAY TWO

Yesterday we looked at the first step to overcoming the emotional stronghold of stress—choosing to rejoice. Now let's see what it means to rejoice and find out how you can do it in your difficult situation.

When reading Paul's command to rejoice, we need to remember the context within which he wrote it. His circumstances certainly didn't offer a reason to rejoice. Remember, rejoicing is not something we do when we're happy—it's a decision we make. We can make this decision because "we know that God causes all things to work together for good to those who love God, to those who are called according to His purpose" (Romans 8:28).

Notice that Paul doesn't say all things *are* good. However, he assures us that God will bring good out of even the worst situation. God causes *all* things to work together for our good.

Let's consider Jesus' most stressful situation. On the eve of His crucifixion, Jesus prayed in the garden that the cup of suffering might pass from Him. There was no happiness associated with dying on a cross.

Jesus was willing to suffer, but He was not eager for it. Your particular "cup" may be a contentious spouse, an overshadowing or overbearing employer, a barren bank account, a chronic health problem, a rebellious child, or some other kind of affliction. Just as Jesus' cup did not pass, neither do many of ours.

So how do we cope? The same way the Lord did, "who for the *joy* set before Him endured the cross" (Hebrews 12:2). Jesus decided to look past the cross, and He saw the glorious plan of God unfolding. The agony and the shame had a purpose. God was working them together for good. Commit yourself to this truth. It will give you new insight so that with eyes of faith, you can see beyond your circumstances and catch a glimpse of God's work in progress.

As long as we expect our circumstances to bring us joy, the best we can hope for are fleeting moments of happiness—and sometimes even less. Your marriage may not be happy, but you can be a joyful spouse. Your job may not be ideal, but you can be a joyful worker. Not every child will rise up and call you blessed, but you can be a joyful parent. But in every case, your joy must be *in the Lord.*

Remember Mary and Martha? We read in Luke 10:38-42 that when the Lord visited their home, Martha labored over a lavish meal while Mary sat at Jesus' feet. Martha asked why the Lord didn't send Mary to the kitchen to help with the preparations.

Martha was feeling the stress! She was angry at Mary for not helping. She was angry at Jesus for allowing Mary to get away with not helping. Martha was a fight waiting to happen, but Jesus disarmed her with His reply. "Martha, you are worried and bothered about so many things, but only one thing is necessary, for Mary has chosen the good part, which shall not be taken away from her."

Let me paraphrase Jesus' words. "Martha, calm down. Take a deep breath and let go of the stress. Settle down and relax. I've got it. Find your joy in Me and not in the meal you're preparing for Me." I can hear that advice echoing still.

"Find your chief joy in Me, pastor, not in the church you're trying to build for Me."

"Find your chief joy in Me, student, not in the grade you're hoping for."

"Find your chief joy in Me, employee, not in your boss's approval."

"Find your chief joy in Me, single person, because no one can fulfill you the way I can."

To rejoice is a choice you must make if you are going to overcome the emotional stronghold of stress.

## DAY THREE

The second step to reduce stress in your life and enjoy more peace is to intentionally live a sensible lifestyle. Immediately after Paul commands the Philippians to rejoice, he writes, "Let your gentle spirit be known to all men. The Lord is near" (Philippians 4:5). The Greek word translated "gentle spirit" or "gentleness" (NIV) can also be translated "reasonableness" (ESV) or "moderation" (KJV). Moderation is not a popular notion in our country. Yet when I travel overseas, I've been amazed at how few fast-food restaurants there are, or junk food dispensers of super-sized candy bars or bags of chips. When you order water or tea, it comes in an eight-ounce glass. Here, people often buy 44 ounces of soda!

In our culture, we shun moderation in other ways too. We're under stress to buy bigger houses, newer cars, or nicer clothes. We dream of grander vacations. So we work harder and longer than ever before, neglecting our need for rest. We try to maintain the image of the perfect Christian home by adding church, midweek meetings, fellowships, outings, athletics, and the like…eventually wondering why we're too stressed out to enjoy any of it.

Trust me, I know busy schedules. As a self-confessed workaholic, I understand what it means to juggle too many things at once. My wife, Lois, has been a God-send in many ways. She has consistently nudged (okay, at times required) me to rest so I can refuel and recharge my body, mind, and spirit.

We all need moderation to reduce stress and enjoy a lifestyle of peace. The next part of the verse we're looking at tells us what happens when we don't. "The Lord is near" when we're living out a gentle lifestyle. God is near even when we're smothered under the weight of too many tasks or too much entertainment, but we become too busy to notice. We drift away from our source of life. And without a sense of God's nearness, we will lack what we need to experience true peace and victory over the emotional stronghold of stress.

The word translated "gentle spirit" also suggests flexibility. Many of us just need to lighten up. Everything's going to be okay. Chill. Nothing generates stress like rigidity. As we encounter life's twists and turns, those who cannot bend will likely break. Resilience is a critical component when handling stress.

Learn to be flexible at work, at home, at school... wherever you are. If somebody irritates you, try not to retaliate—be flexible. If your plans don't work out the way you intended, don't panic—be flexible. If you're facing impossible deadlines, don't give up—be flexible. The world isn't going to end. Tomorrow will be a new day. After all, the Lord is near. When Christ returns, proper justice will be dispensed, all plans will be changed, and all deadlines will be set aside. If you die from a stress-induced heart attack, the same applies. Don't be irresponsible, but be flexible.

To overcome stress, you must schedule times for rest and some recreation. Make sure your to-do list leaves room for the things that are truly important, such as what Mary did—sitting at Jesus' feet and just being with Him. Don't just read His Word and then cross it off your list. Don't use a timer to measure your prayer life. Simply talk to God and listen to what He has to say. Read His Word as though He were speaking to you—because He is.

Spend time in places where you can see and experience the beauty of His creation whether you're with others in a busy city or alone on a nature walk. Simply look up at the sky and appreciate the vast expanse He has made.

Take time for you. This isn't something we learn in our fast-paced, technologically crazed, time-is-money culture. But what are your achievements worth if you can't take time to enjoy them?

Find balance so you can truly experience the peace that comes from knowing the Lord is near.

## DAY FOUR

The final strategy in overcoming the emotional stronghold of stress and obtaining personal peace is to appropriate the power of prayer. "Be anxious for nothing," Paul says, "but in everything by prayer and supplication with thanksgiving let your requests be made known to God" (Philippians 4:6).

In order to get rid of anxiety, one of the major causes of stress, you must fill your mind with something else. That's the way the human brain operates.

Here's an example. Think of the number eight. All right, now *stop* thinking about it. Take the number eight completely out of your mind.

It doesn't work, does it? The harder you try *not* to think about the number eight, the more your thoughts focus on it. Now try this. Think about the number four. Notice how quickly the number eight becomes a distant memory. Two separate thoughts cannot dominate the mind at once.

Enter prayer. The stress of anxiety and apprehension won't burden your life when your mind is filled with prayer.

Why do believers spend so little time praying? Perhaps it has to do with a lack of familiarity and trust. I suspect some Christians hesitate to pray because they spend so little time getting to know the God who hears their prayers. Does He *really* hear? Even if He hears, does He care? Can He help? Only by growing to know the Lord more deeply can we say from experience that His promises are true.

Paul adds the word "supplication." This is just another way of saying, "letting God know what you need." Be specific—name names. Drop the flowery language and complex sentences. Get down to saying what you want to say. I've heard people pray, "Lord, bless me." What does that mean? "Lord, help me at work today." Help you how? Does a coworker annoy you? Have you been assigned a project that seems beyond your capacity? Do you need wisdom? Do you need restraint? Do you just need energy?

Tell Him. Ask Him for what you need. The more explicit your prayers, the more intimate your relationship with God will become—and the more fruit your prayer life will yield.

"But I tried that," you say. "I prayed for a solid week and nothing happened." Chances are, something *has* happened and you failed to see it. God is in the business of answering prayers, not granting wishes. Notice what the passage says—when you pray (verse 6), you get peace (verse 7). There is no guarantee that you will get exactly what you request. God's unfolding plan takes first priority. He is much better at solving our problems than we are.

God may not change your husband right away—He may change you first. Or instead of finding that perfect mate, you may discover some unfinished kingdom business that requires your undivided attention. The project at work may end up a disaster, but you may learn some valuable lessons that will propel you further than you would have gone otherwise.

At times, you may find yourself waiting for God's

timing or God's answer to be revealed. Still, you are promised God's peace.

Prayer and supplication, Paul tells us, should take place within the context of *thanksgiving*. In the midst of praying about your stress and anxieties, Paul suggests giving thanks—which instantly refocuses your attention on the positive side of your circumstances. You might be praying, "Lord, do something about my boss." Thanksgiving adds a new dimension to your prayer: "Lord, I'm thankful You gave me this job. Through this job, You provided the means to buy this home, drive this car, and wear these clothes." In the context of all God is doing, your stress about your boss begins to fade.

The three ingredients we've examined make up God's antidote for stress—far more potent and effective than any pill you can pop, drink you can down, or shopping spree you can splurge on.

But God does more than give you peace. He posts a guard to make sure your peace remains undisturbed. "And the peace of God, which surpasses all comprehension, will guard your hearts and your minds in Christ Jesus" (verse 7). Paul's readers understood this reference clearly. Philippi was a Roman colony, protected from attack and insurrection. God offers us nothing less. The peace of God patrols our heart and mind, shielding us from the enemy's emotional assault and helping us overcome our doubts, insecurities, and fears within.

Many people have tasted this kind of peace, only to watch it slowly evaporate with time. What happened? Did God let down His guard? Of course not. Instead, we walked away from His protection. We left the safe territory God was guarding. We didn't keep our minds stayed on God and His provision. We turned our eyes away from the Solver of our problems and back onto the problems themselves. Don't let that happen to you.

## DAY FIVE

Yesterday we looked at how God shelters your heart and your mind when you turn to Him in your stress. But how can you stay safely within the shelter of God's peace? You do it by changing the way you think. In the next two verses in Philippians 4, Paul tells us how.

> Finally, brethren, whatever is true, whatever is honorable, whatever is right, whatever is pure, whatever is lovely, whatever is of good repute, if there is any excellence and if anything worthy of praise, dwell on these things. The things you have learned and received and heard and seen in me, practice these things, and the God of peace will be with you (verses 8-9).

When you pray, the *peace of God* is with you (verse 7). When you think properly, the *God of peace* is with you (verse 9). God grants His peace when we pray. He helps us sense His presence when we reorient our minds, which also results in peace.

No amount of stress can penetrate God's personal protection. No problem can burst through the shield of His peace and His presence. But living in the security of God's peace requires changing the way you think. Proverbs 23:7 says, "As he thinks within himself, so he is." The things you load into your mind will express themselves in your actions.

There is an old saying in the technological industry— "Garbage in, garbage out." A computer's output will only be as reliable as the programming and data that go into it. The same formula works with people. If you program your mind with stress and anxiety, you shouldn't be surprised to find you're living a stressful life.

How tragic to spend year after year at the mercy of stress while God waits patiently, ready to grant His peace and His presence to any who ask. To overcome the emotional stronghold of stress, we must stop treating the symptoms of stress and seek the cure. We can live above our circumstances rather than under them. Then we'll experience the perfect peace that passes understanding.

## DAY SIX

As we've been discovering how to overcome stress, we've focused on two words—"peace" and "rest." Let's review these before we move on to the next emotional stronghold.

Keep in mind that peace doesn't mean you won't have problems. Peace means your problems won't have you. Jesus said, "In the world you have tribulation" (John 16:33). Relationships may falter. Jobs may be chaotic. Health may decline. The economy could dip, or your personal finances could diminish. "But take courage," says Christ. "I have overcome the world."

Other Bible versions say "take heart" or "be of good cheer." Good cheer? In the midst of stress? How do you do that?

You do it by standing firmly in faith in your connection to Jesus Christ. When you do that, you'll see Him usher in light where there once was darkness. My friend, if He has overcome the world—including your situation—then you have overcome as well in Him. You are an overcomer because He has overcome.

Now let's move on to this second word—"rest." Do you seem to be working harder than ever yet still not getting everything done? We now have access to every possible gadget to make our lives easier and more carefree.

Yet with all this abundance, we often find ourselves burdened with more meetings, more deadlines, and a longer list of things to do.

Jesus tells us the secret to victory over heavy schedules. "Come to Me, all who are weary and heavy-laden, and I will give you rest. Take My yoke upon you and learn from Me, for I am gentle and humble in heart, and you will find rest for your souls" (Matthew 11:28-29).

If Jesus made this promise an app and called it iYoke, would we all download the latest version? Would we access then what we don't access now? His promise—Christ's iYoke—is downloadable through intimate abiding in Him. By wearing Christ's yoke in faith, you will find rest in Him.

Jesus ties His promise of tranquility in the midst of trials to our connection with Him. He promised to leave His peace with us (John 14:27) and dispense it to us as we need it.

This promise doesn't enable us to avoid troubles but to overcome them by being connected to Christ. God often becomes most real to you when He meets you in your emotional distress and empowers you to rise above it rather than sink beneath it. By pursuing intimacy with Christ and His truth, you will discover the rest and the peace you need to overcome the emotional stronghold of stress.

## DAY SEVEN

### Prayers and Practicals

*Dear Father, I've given in to the pressures and
stresses around me for too long. They have
sapped my peace and kept me from enjoying
all You have for me. I admit I sometimes pack
my schedule too full and forget to make time
to be with You or to simply be quiet. I confess
this to You and ask for Your forgiveness. I also
ask that You will enable me to take practical
steps to reduce the stress in my life. Help me
abide in You and develop a habit of rest.*

### Prayer Needs and Requests

_____

_____

_____

_____

_____

_____

*My Own Prayer*

_____

_____

_____

_____

_____

_____

*Practicals*

1. Listen to the online sermon "The Importance of
   Gratitude" at www.youtube.com/watch?v=hYsXq
   ysRXig.

2. Spend some time each day in prayer with the Lord.
   Begin by giving thanks. Write down the things
   you're grateful for and put the list someplace where
   you can look at it when you start feeling stressed.

3. Slow down. Can you cut back on activities? Eat at
   home more often? Watch less TV? Give yourself
   a break from technology and noise so your stress
   can drain away in the stillness. This week, choose
   one activity you can do without and replace it
   with a time of quietness. Go for a walk, sit and
   watch nature, or put out a bird feeder and watch
   the birds. Listen to soft music, meditate, or just
   be still before the Lord.

# WEEK THREE

## WORRY

## DAY ONE

Many struggles in your life can become emotional strongholds, holding you hostage and keeping you from wholeheartedly serving and trusting God and experiencing the abundant life He has promised.

One of the most subtle and damaging strongholds is *worry*. Momentary worry isn't the same as the stronghold of worry. When worry is a stronghold, it's become a way of life, an orientation.

People who are prone to worry have an unlimited supply of things to worry about. Finances, health, and body image. Yesterday, today, and tomorrow. And don't even think about watching the evening news, or you'll have a new list of things to worry about each day.

People cope with worry in various ways. Some people distract themselves by drinking excessively, shopping impulsively, or browsing the Internet incessantly. But none of these remedies do any long-term good because our troubled thoughts quickly return.

Jesus addressed worry head-on. He said not to do it.

In Matthew 6, He said three times, "Do not worry" (verses 25,31,34). The Greek word translated "worry" comes from a root meaning "strangle" or "choke." That's what worry does—it chokes you and prevents you from functioning to the fullest. It leaves you frustrated when you ought to be free.

Friend, worry is one of the most blatant sins because it reveals doubt in God's power and goodness. Some people don't identify their worry as sin. They say they're just concerned about something. However, legitimate concern is different from worry. When you're legitimately concerned about a matter, you're in control. When you worry, the matter controls you. Worry becomes interest paid on trouble before it's due. In reality, roughly 80 percent of the things people worry about never even happen.

Jesus said that because you are His disciple, you can and should stop worrying.

> Do not be worried about your life, as to what you will eat or what you will drink; nor for your body, as to what you will put on. Is not life more than food, and the body more than clothing? Look at the birds of the air, that they do not sow, nor reap nor gather into barns, and yet your heavenly Father feeds them. Are you not worth much more than they? (Matthew 6:25-26).

When we worry, we have forgotten who our Father is. The Lord, who clothes and feeds the birds of the air, surely values us more than birds. He is our Creator and our caring Father. Also, when we worry, we focus on the wrong things. We worry about what we're going to eat and wear when we should focus on the kingdom of God and His righteousness.

Remember His promise that He will never leave you nor forsake you. This is your first antidote to worry.

## DAY TWO

The first lesson we've learned from Matthew 6:25-26 is that if we're bound by the emotional stronghold of worry, we have forgotten who our Father is. Jesus reminds us that we are more valuable than the birds and flowers.

In verse 24, Jesus had just said, "No one can serve two masters; for either he will hate the one and love the other, or he will be devoted to one and despise the other. You cannot serve God and wealth." Then He transitions by saying, "For this reason…"

If money is your master, you're going to worry about it—or the lack of it. If God is your master, then money can't be. In fact, whatever you worry about is usurping God's place as the master of your life.

Jesus put worry in perspective when He asked, "Who of you by being worried can add a single hour to his life?" (verse 27). Worry is like a rocking chair—it can make you feel as if you're moving, but it can't take you anywhere. If we do all we can do and then trust the outcome to God, worry is pointless. We don't need to stay up all night worrying because God stays up all night for us.

To worry is to question God's integrity. Jesus said that the Gentiles—the people who did not know God—were concerned with these things. People who have a relationship with Him shouldn't live or think the same way as those who don't trust in God. God is insulted when we let our worries dominate us and keep us from living as His trusting children.

Lois and I have a getaway spot where we like to escape the hustle and bustle of city life. When I wake up in the mornings out there, I often hear birds singing outside my window. These birds have no bank account, no mutual funds, and no career paths. Yet they are singing away, full of peace and joy. That's what a worry-free life looks like.

Have you ever known someone who kept the bird feeder stocked but wouldn't feed their own kids? Neither have I. God feeds the birds, yet they have no eternal value to Him. But you have so much value to Him that He gave His only Son to purchase your salvation and redemption from hell.

You may have been raised in a situation where your

needs were not met while the needs of those around you were. Or maybe you experienced betrayal in a close relationship or even a marriage. Difficult situations in the past can evoke fresh thoughts of worry, dread, and doubt. But Jesus made a distinction—He's talking about your heavenly Father, not other people. He is a *good* Father who has promised not to neglect you or forsake you. When you remember that God is not like imperfect fathers, you will be on your way to overcoming worry.

## DAY THREE

There are two days you should never spend a lot of time thinking about—yesterday and tomorrow. God doesn't want us worrying about the past or the future. He gives us grace one day at a time. "So do not worry about tomorrow; for tomorrow will care for itself. Each day has enough trouble of its own" (Matthew 6:34).

There once was a man whose family had a history of cancer, and he began to worry that one day, he too would receive the dreaded diagnosis. He worried about it for 30 years—and then suddenly died of a heart attack!

My friend, worrying wastes your time, and it creates negative self-talk that can affect your emotions and actions.

Should you be concerned about your health? Yes.

Should you make efforts to eat wisely and exercise? Yes. Should you manage your money well? Yes. But to worry about issues like these will prevent you from enjoying what you already have. And it won't change your situation one bit.

Jesus told us how to get rid of the kind of worry He forbids—we must change our priorities. "Seek first His kingdom and His righteousness, and all these things will be added to you" (verse 33). When we worry, we are seeking the wrong things. But when we seek God and His kingdom, everything we need falls into place.

If you're prone to struggle with the stronghold of worry, try making a worry box. Just cut a slot in the top of an old shoebox. When you're tempted to worry, write the issue on a slip of paper. Tell the Lord you believe He is able to take care of the worries in your box. You can't handle them, but you know He can. Then fold up your worry, drop it in the box, and leave it to Him. He promises to give you a peace that only He can give, a peace that passes understanding.

Will a worry box make your problems go away? Probably not. But it will shift the weight of those problems from you to God. He is strong enough to carry that burden for you. Let Him do it as you pray something like this.

> *Lord, these are my biggest concerns right now.*
> *You have told me not to worry, but I need Your*

*help. I need You to take these worries from me and give me wisdom from Your Word regarding these concerns. Show me. Guide me. Direct me. Lead me. I can't handle these burdens anymore, but I know You can. Free me up so I can rejoice in You and Your goodness in my life. Thank You, Father—I trust in You.*

## DAY FOUR

America has a problem with identity theft. Technological innovation and online commerce have added to this crisis. People use other people's credit scores and bank accounts to pretend they're someone they're not.

A similar thing happens when we worry too much about what other people think about us. We may try to imitate other successful people rather than simply being who God made us to be. Worrying about other people's acceptance is one of the greatest strongholds a person will have to overcome. People-pleasing strongholds can lead to other problems, such as perfectionism, working too much, and obsessing about body image. What causes people-pleasing strongholds?

When the apostle Paul challenged some misguided leaders, he said, "Am I now seeking the favor of men, or of God? Or am I striving to please men? If I were still trying to please men, I would not be a bond-servant of Christ" (Galatians 1:10). Paul didn't want to be more people-oriented than God-oriented. Our primary goal should be to please God rather than people. Proverbs 29:25 says, "The fear of man brings a snare, but he who trusts in the LORD will be exalted."

Satan distorts our legitimate need for acceptance, tempting us to live behind the mask of a false identity. Some people feel significant only when they please everyone around them. One minute they're trying to please one person, and the next minute they're trying to please someone else. They look for people who pump them up and make them feel good. Left alone, they become depressed.

If you worry about other people's opinion of you, take heart. You *can* overcome this stronghold—but only when you shift your priorities. When you decide that what God says about you is more important than what others think, you can stop seeking other people's approval and start feeling good about God's love for you.

God says you're already accepted, so the acceptance you receive from people is a bonus. Rest in your Father's approval and care. Don't waste your energy trying to win the approval of others. That will drain the life out of you.

Are you driven by people's approval? Remember that their knowledge is incomplete and their emotions are shifting. The God who does not change loves you with an everlasting love that you can count on forever. He has seen your ugly cry, your bad-hair days, and your morning face without makeup. He has heard your rants and raves…yet He loves you more than words can say. That's a love worth embracing.

## DAY FIVE

Perhaps you can relate to the story of Hannah, Samuel's mother. If anyone had a reason to worry, Hannah did. She was one of Elkanah's two wives. She could not conceive children, but Peninnah, the other wife, could. Keep in mind that in ancient Israel, the ability to bear children was critical. As you aged, your children took care of you. To be barren was nearly akin to being cursed. Hannah felt ashamed, and Peninnah's stinging words didn't help. "[Peninnah] would provoke her bitterly to irritate her" (1 Samuel 1:6).

Hannah's pain drove her to tears—and to cry out to God in desperation.

Elkanah and his family traveled to Shiloh every year to sacrifice to the Lord. This was most likely the saddest day of the year for Hannah, yet she was faithful and continued to worship the Lord and seek His presence.

Have you been in a position like this? You worry, you pray in desperation…and nothing changes. Every year

Hannah went to Shiloh as a childless woman. Every year she endured the same taunts. Every year she watched those around her enjoy their children, knowing that someday their offspring would care for them.

Surely Hannah entertained doubts at this time. Would Elkanah continue to love her? Why didn't God answer her prayers? Was she to end up destitute in her old age? She kept trusting and believing and hoping, but nothing happened.

Hannah persevered in her struggles and overcame her worries through prayer and worship. Year after year, she continued to trust and believe that God would act. From the beginning, God knew of her pain and her longing. His silence must not be perceived as inattentiveness or lack of involvement. Friend, when God is silent, He is not still. He does some of His best work when we don't think He is doing a thing.

He was at work in Hannah's situation, but she didn't know it. God was preparing her to give back to Him the very thing she wanted most—her son. Had He answered her prayers early on, Hannah would have had her child and gone on her merry way. But God had a special plan for Hannah's son, Samuel. He was to be a great prophet. Yet the only way Hannah would be moved to this place of surrender was through her painful barrenness. Eventually, Hannah told the Lord she would give Him her son if He would open her womb, which He did. In fact, He did more than that. As Hannah kept her vow and gave

Samuel to the Lord, God gave Hannah five more children (1 Samuel 2:21).

Friend, if you're worried about something right now, consider going to the Lord and giving it back to Him. He often waits for you to trust Him before He moves. This is because fulfilling His purpose and plan in your life is far more important to Him than fulfilling your every whim. He is a wise and gracious God who knows what's best for you and those you love.

## DAY SIX

Have you been completely alone in the dark recently? Your mind can begin to play tricks on you, and before you know it, the hair on the back of your neck is standing on end.

However, if you have a flashlight with you, your fears quickly fade because the light exposes the truth about the darkness. It reveals that there's nothing to fear—your worrisome imagination had created something out of nothing.

In Psalm 23, David wrote about a time when he was sure he was going to lose his life. He had to walk "through the valley of the shadow of death" (verse 4). Yet he wasn't afraid because he knew that the One who illumines the darkest situation was walking with him every step of the way. David traded his worry for faith.

When difficulties in your life tempt you to worry, turn to God's reassuring and never-ending love. When you awake in the middle of the night and sense the enemy whispering, *You're not going to make it through this challenge*, remind yourself of God's truth—Christ has overcome, so you are also an overcomer. Simply proclaim what you know to be true. Shine light on Satan's dark lies.

In essence, David said, "Though my life is in danger, I will not fear because You, my Lord and Savior, are beside me." No force is greater than God. He is the One who loves you with an intimate, personal love. Life may become dark at times, but His light continues to burn. No darkness in this universe is strong enough to quench the light of God's love. You have no reason to worry because God is with you—always.

Have you ever seen a dog that barks at everything whether it's a threat or not? Your brain can be like that, signaling danger whether it's real or imagined. Your mind has been programmed to respond this way, and this was especially helpful during times of great danger in the early years of mankind. But now, when these worry signals appear, you need to assess them and take appropriate action. Is the danger real or imagined? If there's no real basis for it, let it go. Set it aside. If there's no action you can take toward alleviating it, simply turn your thoughts to something else.

On the other hand, some threats are as real as the ones David faced in the valley of darkness. But you can overcome these threats by trading worry for trust that God is with you, trust that He is in control, and trust that you don't have to be afraid. Like David, turn your focus on God and watch your fears turn to praise. David wrote in Psalm 34:3-5, "O magnify the LORD with me, and let us exalt His name together. I sought the LORD, and He answered me, and delivered me from all my fears. They looked to Him and were radiant, and their faces will never be ashamed."

## DAY SEVEN

### Prayers and Practicals

*Dear Father, grant me the serenity to accept the things I cannot change, the courage to change the things I can, and the wisdom to know the difference. Help me to live in the present rather than worry about the future. When my mind starts wandering to things that it shouldn't, bring me back to the present. Free me from the burden of worry and increase my faith in You.*

*Prayer Needs and Requests*

_____

_____

_____

_____

_____

_____

*My Own Prayer*

_____

_____

_____

_____

_____

*Practicals*

1. Think of a problem that a friend or family member worries about. In one column, write down how they are thinking, feeling, and acting and the potential outcome. Then in another column, regarding the same problem, write down your own thoughts, feelings, and actions and the

potential outcome. Notice how thoughts can affect outcomes. Now apply this to something you worry about—compare your thoughts, feelings, actions, and potential outcomes with those of someone who doesn't struggle in this area.

2. Practice breathing calmly. Breathing has far more power than most of us realize. Women have gone through labor without medication simply by mastering the art of focusing and breathing. Breathing deeply can lower your blood pressure, balance your pH levels, and reduce the amount of cortisol flooding your body. That's why you will often hear someone say, "Take ten deep breaths" to someone who is becoming agitated. Set aside time to practice deep breathing on a regular basis, and you'll be more inclined to apply this method to overcoming worry when it strikes.

3. Evaluate your worrisome thoughts. If a thought is not productive or plausible, write it down and stick it in the worry box you made earlier in the week. Pray to the Lord to handle it and to give you His perspective on the matter.

# WEEK FOUR

## HOPELESSNESS

### DAY ONE

A man frantically rushed into his house and told his wife, "We've got a huge problem!"

Calmly she asked, "What is it?"

"There's water in the carburetor of the car, and it won't run," he replied.

"Water is in the carburetor?" She paused…her husband always took their car to the shop when it needed repair. "Honey," she said softly, "I didn't know you knew what a carburetor is. How are you sure there's water in it?"

A look of helplessness drifted over her husband's face. "Because the car is in the swimming pool."

You may never have experienced something as drastic as this, but I'm sure you've faced a seemingly hopeless situation. You probably felt like giving up—maybe on a situation, a job, a relationship…or even on yourself. Moments of hopelessness hit us all. But when hopeless thoughts stick with us and become our normal way of thinking, we have a stronghold.

If you're there right now, remember the message of the cross. Things may appear hopeless (and it can't get any more hopeless than the Son of God dying on a cross), but God can give you back what you have lost. When you hope in Him, He can turn things around.

You can go a long way in life if you have hope. When you feel as though you have nothing else, hope will see you through every difficulty. As believers, we have a tremendous reason to hope. We are assured of God's love for us, and He's done everything in His awesome power to make that love available anytime and anywhere. He even put His Son on the cross so He could give us hope. All we have to do is ask Him to give us the hope we need. He understands the pressures we feel and knows exactly what we need. But the first step to having an overcoming hope is to identify with and abide in "Christ in you, the hope of glory" (Colossians 1:27).

Is your life characterized by your struggles or by hope? Notice how David refers to his past failures and the struggles he once faced. "O Lord my God, I cried to You for help, and You healed me…You have kept me alive, that I would not go down to the pit. Sing praise to the Lord, you His godly ones, and give thanks to His holy name…Weeping may last for the night, but a shout of joy comes in the morning" (Psalm 30:2-5). David knew what it meant to weep. But he also knew what it meant to hope.

If you're struggling with a situation that seems hopeless, you're not alone. Christ, your Savior, is right beside you. As you pray to Him, open your heart to His Word. Hear Him comfort you by giving you hope.

Nothing we face is beyond His ability to heal and restore. Never give up. Sometimes our breakthroughs are delayed because God is waiting to see whether we will turn to Him or we will keep trying to fix our situation ourselves—to somehow drive our car right back out of the pool. But when we put our hope in God, He moves in our lives in a mighty way. Trust Him. The same God who raised Jesus from the grave can resurrect things in your life that had died. Hope can change everything.

## DAY TWO

I often hear people say, "God will not put more on me than I can bear."

Let's debunk that myth right now. In 2 Corinthians 1:8, Paul wrote, "We do not want you to be unaware, brethren, of our affliction…we were burdened excessively, beyond our strength, so that we despaired even of life."

If ever there was an unbearable situation, Paul was in it. And Paul hadn't done anything to cause it. In fact, he had followed God's leading straight into a place of despair. If you share similar feelings today, you're in good company.

God sometimes allows painful situations in your life to accomplish His greater purpose for you. He may be directing your focus onto Him. He wants you to learn the power that comes from living in dependence on Him so you can accomplish everything God has for you to do.

Paul reveals this very key principle in his next statement. "Indeed, we had the sentence of death within ourselves so that we would not trust in ourselves, but in God who raises the dead...*He on whom we have set our hope*" (verses 9-10).

In order to take Paul deeper in faith, God put him in a situation in which his résumé, abilities, and connections were of no value. Why? So that Paul would learn to trust God at a deeper level. Hopelessness is a lot like that. No amount of money in your bank account can buy your way out of it. You can't soothe your way out of it by drinking, eating, or taking drugs. You can't educate your way out of it or adrenaline-rush your way out of it. When each of those momentary pleasures has subsided, you'll find your situation hasn't improved. Hope comes only through trusting that God is sovereign and that He will empower you to pass through the mess of the past and the chaos of today and enter into a fruitful tomorrow.

But keep in mind that the trial, offense, or pain does not make you mature—it's your trust in God in the middle of these situations that makes the difference. When you trust in God in the midst of the pain and align your heart, actions, and thoughts under His Word and truths—that's when you discover the deeper meaning behind the pain.

When we harbor hopelessness and doubt, questioning the pain God allows in our lives, we don't benefit from the trial. We short-circuit our development and thwart the growth process. On the other hand, we experience spiritual growth and maturity when we persevere through pain. That's when our spiritual muscles become strong enough to live the life of faith God has called us to in Jesus Christ.

## DAY THREE

Hope can take you a long way. When I counsel people struggling with emotional strongholds, I check their hope meter. If you've lost your hope, you've lost everything. Hope is the belief that tomorrow will be better than today.

The psalmists knew about the power of hope when life looked hopeless. Psalm 42:1 says, "As the deer pants for the water brooks, so my soul pants for You, O God." Without reading further into the psalm, everything sounds okay. But it's not. Verse 3 says, "My tears have

been my food day and night." Friend, when your tears
are your food day and night, that means you're suffering
from hopelessness and despair. The psalmist is depressed,
and his soul is discouraged.

Yet in his despair, he remembers the Lord. "The LORD
will command His lovingkindness" (verse 8). God has
not yet done it, but the psalmist is confident that He will.
So he talks to himself. He writes to himself—he journals
about his faith in God.

When life crumbles around you, when your friends
aren't talking to you or are telling you the wrong things,
you need to speak to yourself. Look at yourself in the mirror and speak God's truth. Write notes to yourself and
leave them in places where you'll see them. Encourage
yourself. This is what the psalmist did.

He asks himself, "Why are you in despair, O my soul?
And why have you become disturbed within me?" He
doesn't deny his pain or avoid it. Rather, he addresses it
and tells himself what to do. "Hope in God, for I shall
yet praise Him, the help of my countenance and my God"
(verse 11).

What changed the psalmist's feelings of hopelessness
and discouragement? He looked in a different direction.
He looked at what God was going to do even though
he couldn't see it at the time. In other words, he looked
by faith.

The way to overcome the emotional stronghold of
despair, depression, or hopelessness is to fast-forward

through the tough times. Look up ahead to the end. Look toward the place where you surrender your thoughts to the love, grace, and faithfulness of God.

When you do that, the painful situation will no longer own you. Whatever is going wrong will not have the last word. Remember that Satan may have a word, the doctor may have a word, your job, friends, or spouse may have a word…but God always has the final word.

In Lamentations 3, Jeremiah was nothing short of depressed. But instead of wallowing in his misery, he remembered God. When he began to turn his thoughts toward the goodness of God—in spite of the fact that he couldn't see God's goodness at the moment—he started to feel differently about the mess he was in. In fact in Lamentations 3:18, Jeremiah lets us know that he has lost all hope. And yet we see his hope return when he redirects his thoughts toward God.

> Remember my affliction and my wandering, the wormwood and bitterness. Surely my soul remembers and is bowed down within me. This I recall to my mind, therefore I have hope. The LORD's lovingkindnesses indeed never cease, for His compassions never fail. They are new every morning; great is Your faithfulness. "The LORD is my portion," says my soul, "Therefore I have hope in Him" (Lamentations 3:19-24).

Friend, God can touch your mess and make a miracle if you put your hope in Him. He promises, "Those who hopefully wait for Me will not be put to shame" (Isaiah 49:23). God can do more than merely bring you out of your emotional bondage. He can even cause you to forget how deep it was.

Your hopelessness may seem overwhelming, and you may wonder how you'll ever overcome it. But if you will do as Abraham did, who believed "in hope against hope" (Romans 4:18), God will honor your trust. He can and will turn your emotional pain into victorious gain.

## DAY FOUR

Sometimes following Jesus can take us directly into the heart of a storm of hopelessness. That's what happened to Jesus' disciples on the Sea of Galilee. They were simply doing what they had been told to do and wound up in one of the worst nights of their lives. "Immediately He made the disciples get into the boat and go ahead of Him to the other side" (Matthew 14:22).

The disciples were just being obedient, but then winds began pounding their boat, threatening to destroy them. "The boat was already a long distance from the land, battered by the waves" (verse 24).

Have you ever felt blown about or battered even though you were doing exactly what you believed God told you to do? I know I have. I wish I could tell you that when you follow Jesus, you'll never have to face any more storms. But the Bible is full of stories about people who faced hard times while doing exactly what God wanted them to do.

When the Israelites left Egypt and reached the Red Sea, Pharaoh and his army were behind them. Water stretched for miles in front of them. They were stuck even though they had gone exactly where God had sent them. They discovered, as many others have discovered through the centuries, that you can be in the center of God's will and still be stuck in a seemingly hopeless situation.

But God was with them. When you're in trial or a situation that seems hopeless, never think that God is absent or His purposes will not come to pass. He is with you, and He will accomplish His purposes for you. He has a reason for the storms He allows in your life. God sometimes allows trials into our lives in order to reveal Himself to us in a new way. But the benefit we receive from these trials depends largely on how we view them and how we respond to God in the middle of them.

Being in a trial is never fun. But you don't have to go through it alone. A downturn in the economy may put pressure on your financial life. Maybe you've lost your job through no fault of your own. Or maybe these pressures have increased the strain at home and you're facing a storm in your marriage or with your kids.

Wherever and whatever your storm may be, you are not alone. Jesus is with you, and He will see you through. Listen for His voice. Look for Him. If your troubles ever make you feel as if you're drowning, remember that your Lifeguard walks on water.

## DAY FIVE

Hopelessness often comes when we feel we've hit rock bottom. But as I always like to point out, God may let us hit rock bottom in order for us to discover that He is the Rock at the bottom. Hopelessness is often born of times of difficulty, defeat, and discouragement. These seasons are painful, but they are sometimes necessary. The Lord uses our suffering to strip us of our self-sufficiency, to strengthen us, and to help us grow.

Friend, we shouldn't run from difficulties or ignore the lessons to be learned. I understand that trials are not pleasant. They don't make us happy. But if we cooperate with the work God is doing in us, the trials will produce in us a better life than we ever imagined. Jesus said, "Blessed are the poor in spirit, for theirs is the kingdom of heaven" (Matthew 5:3). Those who are spiritually

broken will be blessed because they will experience kingdom life in a special way. They will experience God's presence flowing through their lives in a uniquely personal
manner.

Scripture promises that God remains close to those
who are broken and makes them stronger than before.
Psalm 34:18 says, "The LORD is near to the broken-
hearted and saves those who are crushed in spirit." Isaiah
61:3 teaches that God gives those who mourn "a garland
instead of ashes, the oil of gladness instead of mourning,
the mantle of praise instead of a spirit of fainting. So they
will be called oaks of righteousness, the planting of the
LORD, that He may be glorified."

We've all seen restored furniture. Restoring furniture
involves stripping away old varnish or paint with strong
chemicals. This reveals all the nicks and scratches in the
wood. Next, the wood is sanded to smooth out its imperfections. Then the furniture is ready to receive a new stain
or coat of paint. It's ready for a new look.

New glory can be given to old furniture. And God
can do the same thing with you. He can put new glory
inside your old life, but He must first strip away the
blemishes and sand away the rough spots to bring you to
a place of purity and dependence on Him.

The Lord longs to bless you, but He also wants to
transform and restore you. Sometimes the greatest path
to healing involves embracing the hurt, trusting that
God is after your greater good. Just as an athlete endures

painful workouts to get to the next level, God often uses pain in our lives to make us stronger.

Today, thank Him for what He is doing through the trials you're facing. You might not be ready to thank Him for the trials themselves, but you can thank Him for the good He is producing through them. Do it even if you don't feel like it. Do it by whatever amount of faith you have right now.

## DAY SIX

You exist for God. You are His special creation. He formed you because He loves you. The reason you are to get up each and every morning is to fulfill God's purpose for your life. And it is a great purpose—a wonderful purpose. In fact, according to Jeremiah 29:11, *God has a good plan just for you.*

The God who created you for Himself has never made any mistakes. His plan for you has no flaws. Yes, you've endured trials. And there will be more in the years ahead. But these difficult trials will work together for good if you love God, draw near to God, and experience God. He promises.

God's Word tells us, "In all these things, we overwhelmingly conquer through Him who loved us"

(Romans 8:37). The most important word in that verse is often overlooked. I must have preached on that verse a hundred times in the past 40 years, but I never saw it until just recently. I was applying this passage to my own life recently, and God seemed to mark this word with a yellow highlighter and make it come alive.

You might think "conquer" or "overwhelmingly" is the most important word. Actually, I don't think so. I'd say the most important word is "in." We are often tempted to believe that God promised to keep us *from* difficulties in life, and when He doesn't, we feel discouraged.

But God never promised to deliver us *from* all things. He has promised that "*in* all these things" we will overwhelmingly conquer. We will receive the benefits and blessings that come only through our deep and meaningful experience of Him.

Friend, this powerful principle has warmed and strengthened my heart, and I want it to warm and strengthen yours too. Life is too important and too short to miss out on all that God has for you. But that's exactly what happens when we focus on the mess rather than the truth of God's Word. God has never promised to keep us from our problems, but He has promised to make us victors who overwhelmingly conquer while *in* them. Change your perspective, and you will change your life.

Jeremiah lived this way. If anyone had a reason to be bound in emotional turmoil, he did. His city was destroyed. His people were falling apart. His future looked bleak. Yet in spite of it all, he praised God's faithfulness.

You too can praise Him because you will overwhelmingly conquer in your current situation if you will simply look to God as your source and your strength. Ask Him to fill your heart with confidence that those who hope in God will never be put to shame (Psalm 25:3 NIV). In other words, hope in God, and you will never regret that you did.

## DAY SEVEN

### Prayers and Practicals

*Dear Father, I want to hope in You. I believe in You—help my unbelief. Speak to me, and help me to hear and discern Your voice. Revive my hope, and help me see Your presence and control in my life. Give me glimpses of hope where there are none. Where I am tempted to give up, help me to reengage—in my marriage, at work, in my relationships, or in any other struggle. Show me steps to take to hope again and make a new start.*

*Prayer Needs and Requests*

_____

_____

_____

_____

_____

_____

*My Own Prayer*

_____

_____

_____

_____

_____

_____

*Practicals*

1. Make an intentional effort to walk three to five times a week for a minimum of 20 minutes. If you are unable to do this, find a gym and exercise for that long. It is amazing how your perspective can change when your body is healthier and more active. The same goes for food—be sure

you eat foods that contribute to your well-being and mental clarity rather than junk or processed foods that can weigh you down physically. Find an inexpensive juicer and make a habit of juicing and drinking brain-stabilizing foods, such as spinach, strawberries, and pineapples.

2. Remember that your problems will not be solved overnight. God often brings us through times of trial (what I call the wilderness) in order to strengthen our faith. When your problems don't just go away, learn how to wait well by...

   * affirming God's faithfulness through what you say, think, and do

   * spending time with Him in prayer and worship

   * resisting the temptation to complain, gossip, whine, and resort to laziness or overindulgence

3. Choose to intentionally memorize Scripture verses of hope. Keep a list of them in a location you can find them easily, and routinely put these truths into your mind. Speak them out loud. Insert your name in them or make them first-person when you can. Most of all, trust God's truth.

# CONCLUSION

## DAY TWENTY-NINE

Once upon a time, an eagle egg was nudged out of its nest and rolled down the side of the mountain, finally coming to a rest in the middle of a turkey farm. Still a little dizzy, a newborn eaglet wiggled out of his broken shell and looked around at the big, wide world.

Naturally, the little guy had no idea he was an eagle. As time went by, he concluded that he was just a scrawny, funny-looking turkey. Soon, he began to adopt the mannerisms of those around him. He pecked at the grain in the barnyard, bobbed his head with the best of them, and even managed a pitiful-sounding gobble from time to time.

One day, a flock of eagles flew overhead. The young, would-be turkey looked at them longingly, admiring their graceful flight. As he watched them fly by, one of the passing birds glanced down at the barnyard with his sharp eagle eyes, hardly believing what he saw. He swooped down, landed next to the young eaglet and said, "What in the world are you doing here?"

"This is where I was born," the youngster replied. "This is my home."

The great bald eagle snapped back, "This may be where you were born, but your home is in the sky. Don't you know who you are? Spread out those wings and fly!"

Sure enough, the young eaglet extended his wings. A surge of excitement raced through him when he felt himself being lifted skyward. As he left the ground, one of the turkeys caught sight of him and asked, "Where are you going?"

"I'm going to be who I was created to be," he replied. In no time, he was soaring toward the clouds.

.........

God created you to be an eagle, soaring on the wind of His Holy Spirit. He gave you wings strong enough to carry you, steady and sure, through the storms of life. He gave you sharp eyes, capable of focusing clearly on His divine perspective.

How tragic to settle for life as a turkey when the open sky awaits you. Yet that is exactly what will happen if you remain in emotional bondage. Rather than live a defeated life, controlled by your disordered thoughts and habits, isn't it time to live according to what God says about you? He says you have a future full of hope. He says you are fearfully and wonderfully made. He says you are loved, you are an overcomer, and you can overwhelmingly conquer all that life throws at you. He says you are His and He will never leave you.

Friend, may your days ahead be greater than your days gone by, and as you learn and apply God's truths, may they give you the wings to soar high.

## DAY THIRTY

Most baby boomers remember Popeye the Sailor Man. Popeye was often brutalized by Brutus, the bully who sought to wreak havoc on Popeye's life. One of his favorite tricks was to steal Popeye's girlfriend, Olive Oyl.

Brutus was always beating up Popeye. Finally, when poor Popeye couldn't take it any longer, he would reach for a can of spinach. After opening it and downing the contents, things changed quickly. The spinach made Popeye strong—so strong, in fact, that Brutus became the victim and no longer the victor. He was now subject to Popeye's new infusion of power, and for a while at least, Popeye was on top. However, you knew that by the time the next Popeye cartoon began, he would be losing to Brutus all over again until he reached for another can of spinach.

Many people are regularly beaten by their own Brutuses—circumstances or other people who cause pain. Maybe you suffer under the weight of worry, stress, or hopelessness. Some days, the sorrow and heartache never seem to end. However, I hope that during our 30 days together, you've learned some powerful truths and principles that will help you deal with life's burdens. Use the heathy responses you've learned rather than opening a bottle of alcohol, taking a chemical substance, or employing any number of unhealthy ways to cope with pain. Those things only provide a temporary relief, but God can make you a permanent overcomer.

Dependence on anything but Christ adds even more instability and hopelessness (and perhaps addiction and codependency) to the original root problem.

Jesus knew you would face the burdens and stresses you do. He knew about everything that would happen to you. He saw it all, and He knows the potential it has to overwhelm you and to cause you to shrink back in fear and emotional bondage. That's why He gave you these compassionate words to help you gain your victory over emotional strongholds.

> Come to Me, all who are weary and heavy-laden, and I will give you rest. Take My yoke upon you and learn from Me, for I am

gentle and humble in heart, and you will
find rest for your souls (Matthew 11:28-29).

Do you hear His voice? He is asking you to come. To
take His yoke. And to rest.
Will you?

# ABOUT DR. TONY EVANS

Dr. Tony Evans is founder and senior pastor of the 9500-member Oak Cliff Bible Fellowship in Dallas, founder and president of The Urban Alternative, chaplain of the NBA's Dallas Mavericks, and author of *Destiny* and *Victory in Spiritual Warfare*. His radio broadcast, *The Alternative with Dr. Tony Evans*, can be heard on more than 1000 outlets and in more than 130 countries.

# THE URBAN ALTERNATIVE

Dr. Evans and The Urban Alternative (TUA) equip, empower, and unite Christians to impact *individuals, families, churches,* and *communities* to restore hope and transform lives.

We believe the core cause of the problems we face in our personal lives, homes, churches, and societies is a spiritual one. Therefore, the only way to address them is spiritually. We've tried political, social, economic, and even religious agendas. It's time for a kingdom agenda— God's visible and comprehensive rule over every area of life—because when we function as we were designed, God's divine power changes everything. It renews and restores as the life of Christ is made manifest in our own. As we align ourselves under Him, He brings about full restoration from deep within. In this atmosphere, people are revived and made whole.

As God's kingdom impacts us, it impacts others— transforming every sphere of life. When each sphere of life functions in accordance with God's Word, the outcomes are evangelism, discipleship, and community impact. As we learn how to govern ourselves under God, we transform the institutions of family, church, and society according to a biblically based kingdom perspective. Through Him, we are touching heaven and changing earth.

To achieve our goal, we use a variety of strategies, methods, and resources for reaching and equipping as many people as possible.

## Broadcast Media

Hundreds of thousands of individuals experience *The Alternative with Dr. Tony Evans* through daily radio broadcasts on more than 1000 radio outlets and in more than 100 countries. The broadcast can also be seen on several television networks and online at TonyEvans.org.

## Leadership Training

*Kingdom Agenda Pastors (KAP)* provides a viable network for like-minded pastors who embrace the kingdom agenda philosophy. Pastors have the opportunity to go deeper with Dr. Evans as they are given biblical knowledge, practical applications, and resources to impact individuals, families, churches, and communities. KAP welcomes senior and associate pastors of all churches.

*Kingdom Agenda Pastors' Summit* progressively develops church leaders to meet the demands of the twenty-first century while maintaining the gospel message and the strategic position of the church. The Summit introduces intensive seminars, workshops, and resources, addressing issues affecting the community, family, leadership, organizational health, and more.

*Pastors' Wives Ministry*, founded by Dr. Lois Evans, provides counsel, encouragement, and spiritual resources for pastors' wives as they serve with their husbands in ministry. The ministry focuses on the KAP Summit, which offers senior pastors' wives a safe place to reflect, renew, relax, and receive training in personal development, spiritual growth, and care for their emotional and physical well-being.

## Community Impact

*National Church Adopt-A-School Initiative (NCAASI)* prepares churches across the country to impact communities by using public schools as the primary vehicle for effecting positive social change in urban youth and families. Leaders of churches, school districts, faith-based organizations, and other nonprofit organizations are equipped with the knowledge and tools to forge partnerships and build strong social-service delivery systems. This training is based on the comprehensive church-based community impact strategy conducted by Oak Cliff Bible Fellowship. It addresses such areas as economic development, education, housing, health revitalization, family renewal, and racial reconciliation. We also assist churches in tailoring the model to meet the specific needs of their communities while simultaneously addressing the spiritual and moral frame of reference.

## Resource Development

We are fostering lifelong learning partnerships with the people we serve by providing a variety of published materials. We offer booklets, Bible studies, books, CDs, and DVDs to strengthen people in their walk with God and ministry to others.

.........

For more information, a catalog of Dr. Tony Evans's ministry resources, and a complimentary copy of Dr. Evans's devotional newsletter, call

**(800) 800-3222**

or write

**The Urban Alternative**
**PO Box 4000**
**Dallas TX 75208**

or visit our website:

**www.TonyEvans.org**

# MORE GREAT HARVEST HOUSE BOOKS BY DR. TONY EVANS

### A Moment for Your Soul

In this uplifting devotional, Dr. Evans offers a daily reading for Monday through Friday and one for the weekend—all compact, powerful, and designed to reach your deepest need. Each entry includes a relevant Scripture reading for the day.

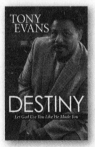

### Destiny

Dr. Evans shows you the importance of finding your God-given purpose. He helps you discover and develop a custom-designed life that leads to the expansion of God's kingdom. Embracing your personal assignment from God will lead to your deepest satisfaction, God's greatest glory, and the greatest benefit to others.

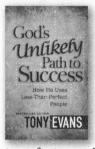

### God's Unlikely Path to Success

Dr. Evans uses prominent Bible characters to show that God delights in using imperfect people who have failed, sinned, or just plain blown it. You'll be encouraged as you come to understand that God has you, too, on a path to success despite your imperfections and mistakes.

### The Power of God's Names

Dr. Evans shows that it's through the names of God that the nature of God is revealed. By understanding the characteristics of God as revealed through His names, you will be better equipped to face the challenges life throws at you.

### Praying Through the Names of God

Dr. Evans reveals insights into some of God's powerful names and provides prayers based on those names. Your prayer life will be revitalized as you connect your needs with the relevant characteristics of His names.

### Victory in Spiritual Warfare

Dr. Evans demystifies spiritual warfare and empowers you with a life-changing truth: Every struggle faced in the physical realm has its root in the spiritual realm. With passion and practicality, Dr. Evans shows you how to live a transformed life in and through the power of Christ's victory.

### 30 Days to Victory Through Forgiveness

Has someone betrayed you? Are you suffering the consequences of your own poor choices? Or do you find yourself asking God, Why did You let this happen? Like a skilled physician, Dr. Evans leads you through a step-by-step remedy that will bring healing to that festering wound and get you back on your journey to your personal destiny.

To learn more about Harvest House books and
to read sample chapters, visit our website:

**www.harvesthousepublishers.com**

**HARVEST HOUSE PUBLISHERS**
EUGENE, OREGON